25 Fun Word Family Songs
Sung to Favorite Tunes

SCHOLASTIC

Easy-to-Learn Songs With Activities
That Target and Teach the Top Word Families

Pamela Chanko

D1225492

New York · Toronto · London · Auckland · Sydney
Mexico City · New Delhi · Hong Kong · Buenos Aires

Teaching *Resources*

Cover design by Jason Robinson
Interior design by Sydney Wright
Cover and interior illustrations by Bari Weissman

ISBN: 978-0-545-44882-6

1 2 3 4 5 6 7 8 9 10   40   19 18 17 16 15 14 13

Contents

The Word Family Songs

Long- and Short-*a* Word Families

Long- and Short-*e* Word Families

Long- and Short-*i* Word Families

Short-*o* Word Families

Short-*u* Word Families

Introduction

From tying their shoes to riding a bike, children just love learning to do things on their own—and one of the most exciting things of all is reading. The thrill on a child's face when he or she is able to put down a book and say, "I read it all by myself!" is enough to warm any teacher's heart. What's more, emergent literacy—the discovery of letters, sounds, and how they work—can be a delightful process in itself. The journey toward becoming a fluent reader is part of the fun; and with *25 Fun Word Family Songs*, that element of playful discovery is applied to its fullest!

The science and research behind the teaching of word families is conclusive: It improves children's decoding skills and sight word vocabulary enormously, leading to increased fluency and comprehension. Think of the words *cat*, *rat*, and *mat*. These words both rhyme and end with the same spelling pattern. The fact that their word endings (or phonograms) both sound and look the same means they all belong to the *–at* word family. And once children learn these simple sound/symbol relationships, they can more easily recognize and read words like *pat*, *sat*, *slat*, *scat*, *flat*, *that*, and *splat*. Research shows that the less time children need to spend on decoding, the more time they have for comprehension—which is, of course, the ultimate goal of literacy.

In addition to being an educationally sound practice, teaching word families is just plain FUN. Children at this stage of learning take delight in rhyming sounds and the musicality of language. That's how the idea of word family songs was born—why not capitalize on that musicality even more by teaching word families to actual music? Singing is already a big part of most early childhood and elementary classrooms, and a favorite one at that. Now you can fit literacy lessons right in! Each catchy, rhyming song in this book teaches one of the top 25 word families—and statistics show that nearly 500 primary-grade words can be formed from a very small group of those families!

What's more, you won't need a CD player or accompanist to sing these ditties; the lyrics to these songs are sung to classic and familiar children's tunes. For instance, "Do You Want to Bake a Cake"? teaches the *–ake* family to the tune of "Twinkle, Twinkle Little Star," while "If You See a Little Duck" teaches the *–uck* family to the tune of "London Bridge Is Falling Down." All you need is a copier to reproduce the song sheets. Pass them out to children, and you'll be ready to go!

Beginning on page 6, you'll find teaching tips for introducing and using the songs as well as activity ideas to extend learning. As a bonus, you'll also find handy reproducible word cards to go with each song sheet. (See pages 34–58.) Simply copy and cut apart, and children will have a word bank that includes each word they've learned while singing!

Now get ready to learn and sing! Enjoy!

25 Fun Word Family Songs Sung to Favorite Tunes © 2013 by Pamela Chanko, Scholastic Teaching Resources

Connections to the Common Core State Standards

The songs and companion activities in this book will help you meet your specific state reading and language arts standards as well as those recommended by the Common Core State Standards Initiative (CCSSI). These materials address the following standards, adapted from the CCSS for English Language Arts, for students in grades K–2. For details on these standards, visit the CCSSI Web site: www.corestandards.org.

Reading Standards for Literature

Key Ideas and Details

RL.K.1, RL.1.1, RL.2.1: Ask and answer questions about key details in a text.

RL.K.2, RL.1.2: Retell stories including key details.

Craft and Structure

RL.K.4: Ask and answer questions about unknown words in a text.

RL.K.5: Recognize common types of texts.

RL.1.4: Identify words and phrases in stories or poems that suggest feelings or appeal to the senses.

RL.2.4: Describe how words and phrases supply rhythm and meaning in a story, poem, or song.

Integration of Knowledge and Ideas

RL.K.7: With prompting and support, describe the relationship between illustrations and the story in which they appear.

RL.1.7: Use illustrations and details in a story to describe its characters, setting, or events.

RL.2.7: Use information from the illustrations and words in a print text to demonstrate understanding of its characters, setting, or plot.

Range of Reading and Level of Text Complexity

RL.K.10: Actively engage in group reading activities with purpose and understanding.

RL.1.10: With prompting and support, read prose of appropriate complexity for grade 1.

Reading Standards: Foundational Skills

Print Concepts

RF.K.1, RF.1.1: Demonstrate understanding of the organization and basic features of print.

Phonological Awareness

RF.K.2, RF.1.2: Demonstrate understanding of spoken words, syllables, and sounds (phonemes).

Phonics and Word Recognition

RF.K.3, RF.1.3, RF.2.3: Know and apply grade-level phonics and word analysis skills in decoding words.

Fluency

RF.K.4, RF.1.4, RF.2.4: Read with sufficient accuracy and fluency to support comprehension.

Language Standards

Conventions of Standard English

L.K.1, L.1.1, L.2.1: Demonstrate command of the conventions of standard English grammar and usage when writing or speaking.

Vocabulary Acquisition and Use

L.K.4, L.1.4, L.2.4: Determine or clarify the meaning of unknown and multiple-meaning words and phrases, choosing flexibly from an array of strategies.

L.K.6, L.1.6, L.2.6: Use words and phrases acquired through conversations, reading and being read to, and responding to texts.

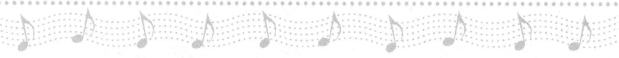

Using the Songs

Use the following teaching tips to get the most out of using the songs with your students. You'll also find ideas on how to use the word cards, phonogram cards, and word-family word lists (pages 34–64), included in this resource.

Before Singing

✿ Make a copy of the song sheet for each child.

✿ Before going over the lyrics, make sure children are familiar with the tune. Sing the song with the original lyrics a few times through, or just hum the tune on its own.

✿ You can preview the new lyrics with children by displaying them on a whiteboard. Track the print when you first read the lyrics with the group.

✿ Before singing the song, introduce the target word family to children. First, point to the letters in the phonogram and say its sound aloud. Have children repeat the sound of the phonogram after you. Then explain that the song will have many words that end with that sound. Try working with the group to list some words from the word family and have them predict which might be in the song, judging by its title.

The lyrics to the songs in this book can be sung to the tunes of familiar and favorite children's songs. You can listen to many of these tunes at the following Web sites.

Free Kids Music
freekidsmusic.com/
traditional-childrens-songs

KIDiddles
kididdles.com/lyrics/
traditional.html

Lyrics & Words for Children's Nursery Rhymes & Songs
bussongs.com/traditional-songs.php

During Singing

✿ The first time you sing each song, you might want to sing it aloud on your own. This will help familiarize children with the words and how they fit into the tune.

✿ The next time you sing, you might want to try echo singing: Sing one line at a time, having children repeat it after you.

✿ Once you're sure the group is familiar with the words and tune, sing the song together straight through. Then sing it again, this time asking children to pay special attention to the words in the word family.

25 Fun Word Family Songs Sung to Favorite Tunes © 2013 by Pamela Chanko, Scholastic Teaching Resources

✿ After helping children identify the word-family words in the song, hand out copies of the word cards that go with that song. (See pages 34–58.) Children can cut them apart and hold up the correct card as they sing each word in the song.

✿ You can also try using a cloze technique. Sing the song and then pause when you come to a word-family word. Children can chime in with the word as they hold up their cards.

✿ Children might also highlight the word-family words on their song sheets. This way, they can more easily match the appropriate card to each word.

✿ As children become more familiar with the songs, invite them to make up simple body and hand movements that help act out or tell the song's story.

✿ Remember that the songs can be sung in a variety of settings. You may choose to sing a song at circle time, morning meeting, snack time, at transitions, or to say goodbye at the end of the school day. You can use the songs to teach word family mini-lessons to the whole class, or in small groups. If different groups are practicing different songs, you might even have a class concert!

After Singing

✿ You can turn any song in the book into a listening center by recording children singing the song themselves! Place the recording in the center along with copies of the song sheets and have children follow along with the recording.

✿ Try using the song sheets as a take-home activity. Children can take the songs home and teach them to family members. Ask parents and other caregivers to work with children to circle each word in the song that belongs to the target word family.

✿ The phonogram cards (59–62) are great for brainstorming new words from each word family. (You can also get ideas from the word-family word lists on pages 63–64, which include words not in the songs themselves.) Simply have children write a new letter (or letters) on the line before the word ending. Then decide on a spot to place the new word in the song. Do this a few times, and you've got a new song with your own silly lyrics!

Extending Learning

Use the reproducible cards (pages 34–62) with these fun word family extension activities.

Shake 'n' Sort

1. Gather a small group to play this game. Assign each child a different word family and put all the word cards from each family in a bag. Have children sit in a circle. The first child picks a card from the bag. If it belongs to his or her word family, the child keeps the card. If not, the card gets returned to the bag.

2. Continue around the circle, each child picking a word card, keeping it only if the word belongs to his or her word family.

3. When the bag is empty, children can read their words aloud—and lead the group in a rendition of the song that goes with their word family!

A Minute to Win It!

1. Gather a small group of children. Give each child three to five copies of the same phonogram cards. (Laminate to make them reusable, if desired.) For instance, you might like to focus on the word endings –at, –ill, and –ug for one game.

2. Give each child a pencil (or erasable marker) and set a timer for one minute. Have children fill in an initial letter (or letters) on the lines to make words on their cards, as many as they can within the time period.

3. When the time is up, have children count how many words they made. Which child made the most words in just one minute?

Silly Sentences

1. Choose a target word family to make up a silly story! Make a copy of the word cards for that word family and several copies of the corresponding phonogram card.

2. First, work with the group to brainstorm additional words, writing an initial letter (or letters) on the line to complete the phonogram cards. Have blank index cards on hand as well, so you can write transitional words.

3. Then work together to use most or all of the words in a silly sentence or two!

Word Family Go Fish

1. Play a word family version of Go Fish. Copy several word card sheets and cut out two cards from each sheet. Then gather a small group to play and deal seven cards to each player. Place the rest of the cards facedown in the middle of the group.

2. Have children take turns asking another player "Do you have a word that rhymes with [one of the words in their hand]?" If the child asked has a rhyming word card, he or she gives it to the player, who then places the pair face up on the table. If not, the child says "Go Fish" and the player takes a card from the center pile.

3. Play continues until all players have matched all their cards.

25 Fun Word Family Songs Sung to Favorite Tunes © 2013 by Pamela Chanko. Scholastic Teaching Resources

Jack's Snack

(sung to "The Hokey Pokey")

There was a boy called Jack
Who reached up to a rack.
He grabbed himself some crackers
And he put them in a stack.
He took some peanut butter
And he spread it all around.
That's how he made a snack!

Now this boy called Jack
He also had a pack.
He put the snack inside it
And he put it on his back.
He zipped it up and fixed the straps
and carried it around.
The snack was in Jack's black pack!

Then this boy called Jack
He saw his friend called Zack.
Zack thought they'd eat together
But his sack was empty—ack!
But Jack had lots of food,
There was enough to go around.
That's how they shared Jack's snack!

Do You Want to Bake a Cake?

(sung to "Twinkle, Twinkle Little Star")

Do you want to bake a cake?
What a cake we're going to make!
Shake in flour, sugar, too,
Then we take an egg or two.
Stir it up and let it bake,
Yum!
That's good, for goodness' sake!

25 Fun Word Family Songs Sung to Favorite Tunes © 2013 by Pamela Chanko, Scholastic Teaching Resources

Stan and Fran's Van

(sung to "The Itsy-Bitsy Spider")

Fran and Stan, they had a plan
To ride inside the van.
Fran told Stan, "Turn on the fan!
This van's a frying pan!"
Stan told Fran, "You're right, it's hot,
But I don't think I can."
The fan was broken, so they called
A handyman named Dan.

Now Dan had a job to do,
So down the street he ran.
Dan told Stan and Fran
That they had called the perfect man!
"If anyone can fix this fan,"
He said, "I know I can."
And so he did, and then all three
Went riding in the van!

The Snap-Tap, Clap-Flap Rap

(sung to "Jingle Bells")

First you snap,
Then you tap,
Then you give a clap.
Then you act just like a bird,
And with your arms you flap—Hey!
Slap your lap,
That's a wrap!
Time to take a nap.
Oh, what fun it is to do
The Snap-Tap, Clap-Flap Rap!

Flash and Crash

(sung to "The Wheels on the Bus")

The lightning in the sky goes flash, flash, flash,
Flash, flash, flash, flash, flash, flash.
The lightning in the sky goes flash, flash, flash,
A storm has come to town.

The thunder in the air goes crash, crash, crash,
Crash, crash, crash, crash, crash, crash.
The thunder in the air goes crash, crash, crash,
A storm has come to town.

The trees and the leaves go thrash, thrash, thrash,
Thrash, thrash, thrash, thrash, thrash, thrash.
The trees and the leaves go thrash, thrash, thrash,
A storm has come to town.

Run and get inside now, dash, dash, dash!
Dash, dash, dash, dash, dash, dash!
Run and get inside now, dash, dash, dash!
A storm has come to town.

Tomorrow in the puddles, we'll splash, splash, splash,
Splash, splash, splash, splash, splash, splash.
Tomorrow in the puddles, we'll splash, splash, splash,
When the storm is gone from town!

Cat, Rat, Gnat!

(sung to "Row, Row, Row Your Boat")

Once I had a cat,
Who was very fat.
But then he sat right on my hat,
And he crushed it flat!

Then I had a rat,
Who was nice to pat.
But then my parents had a chat
And told the rat to scat.

Next, a little gnat
Crawled in through a slat.
But then I heard a tiny *splat*—
And that's the end of that!

25 Fun Word Family Songs Sung to Favorite Tunes © 2013 by Pamela Chanko, Scholastic Teaching Resources

Kate and Tate

(sung to "I'm a Little Teapot")

Kate had a date
To skate with Tate.
But Kate ate her breakfast
At too slow a rate.
Kate was in a state—
Now she was late!
And that was something
Tate would hate!

Kate had an idea
And called up Tate.
She told Tate to wait for her
Right at the gate.
To say she was sorry
That she was late,
She brought him breakfast
On a plate!

A Day to Play

(sung to "When the Saints Come Marching In")

Oh what a day, a day to play!
Just follow me, let's go this way!
We'll have lots of fun all together,
When we all go out to play!

What do you say? The sky is gray?
And maybe rain will start to spray?
We will still have fun all together,
If we all stay in to play!

But look that way! I see a ray!
The sun is out. It's here to stay!
Now let's sing out loud all together:
What a day to play, say:
YAY!

A Treat to Eat

(sung to "Camptown Races")

Let's sit down and have a treat,
Yummy! Yummy!
Let's sit down and have a treat.
Come, let's have a seat.

What's a treat that can't be beat?
Yummy! Yummy!
Something we won't have to heat.
What treat should we eat?

Something simple, something neat,
Yummy! Yummy!
Hey! I know what we will eat!
Apples—what a treat!

Cheep and Peep at the Farm

(sung to "On Top of Old Smokey")

Let's go to the farm now.
We'll drive in the jeep.
We'll see all the animals,
Like horses and sheep.

We'll go to the henhouse,
And hear the chicks peep.
And up in the treetops,
We'll hear the birds cheep.

And out in the garden,
The insects will creep.
We might see a ladybug,
And catch it to keep.

We'll climb up the hillside,
So grassy and steep.
Then jump in the pond,
So cool and so deep.

Get back in the jeep now,
And make the horn beep.
The farm was so busy,
Let's go home and sleep!

18

The Shop in the Dell

(sung to "The Farmer in the Dell")

I have a bell to sell.
My bell is really swell!
Just ring it for attention,
And you'll never have to yell!

I have a shell to sell.
My shell is really swell!
I found it in the ocean,
And it has a beachy smell!

My shop is in the dell.
I'm sure that you can tell,
That in my shop I sell a lot—
And do it very well!

The Best Nest

(sung to "Hush Little Baby")

If you see a robin's nest,
It is best to let it rest.
Do not ever be a pest,
Just let that bird's nest rest!

Look at Robin in her nest,
Folded wings across her chest.
She protects her eggs the best,
In her little nest.

Peck—an eggshell gets a test.
One egg's hatching before the rest.
CRACK! It's open! That's the best—
A new chick's in the nest!

Three Nice Mice

(sung to "Three Blind Mice")

Three nice mice,
Ate some rice.
They put in
Lots of spice.
The mice were so hungry,
They ate rice twice.
And then they each
Bought a pizza slice!
It cost a lot,
But was worth the price,
For three nice mice!

Slide, Glide, and Ride!

(sung to "My Bonnie")

On ice skates I slide and I glide,
Then I build a big snowman, so wide!
The hill by my house is all snowy—
Down its side I am going to ride!

Snow day, let's play!
Don't hide at home, come and take a ride!
Snow day, let's play!
Come out and take a ride!

25 Fun Word Family Songs Sung to Favorite Tunes © 2013 by Pamela Chanko, Scholastic Teaching Resources

My Night-Light

(sung to "Are You Sleeping?")

What's that sight,
Nice and bright?
No more fright.
It's just right.
I'm tucked in nice and tight now.
Can you guess the sight now?
My night-light!
My night-light!

Jill's Dollar Bill

(sung to "Miss Lucy Had a Baby")

Jill went to the store,
She had a dollar bill.
She couldn't find a thing to buy,
So she gave it to Will.

Now Will had the dollar,
It gave him quite a thrill,
He thought he'd buy some candy,
Enough to have his fill.

But candy hurts your tummy,
And that gave Will a chill.
He didn't want the money,
So he gave it to Bill.

Now Bill had the dollar,
And walked on up the hill.
It dropped right to the bottom—oops!
And there it's lying still!

Will You Be a Friend of Mine?

(sung to "Do You Know the Muffin Man?")

Will you be a friend of mine?
Come out to play,
The sun will shine.
Will you be a friend of mine?
It will be so fine.

Will you be a friend of mine?
Come climb a pine,
My yard has nine!
Will you be a friend of mine?
It will be so fine.

Will you be a friend of mine?
Come join the line,
Then come to dine!
Will you be a friend of mine?
It will be so fine.

Sing of Spring!

(sung to "This Old Man")

Let's all sing
For the spring.
It's the time when birds take wing,
And the bees all buzz
But be careful 'cause they sting!
These are all the signs of spring!

Let's all sing
For the spring.
Go outside and ride a swing.
Let your kite fly high,
Just stand back, unroll the string!
These are all the signs of spring!

Let's all sing
For the spring.
Butterflies on flowers cling,
And the grass grows green,
It is such a lovely thing!
These are all the signs of spring!

The School Clock

(sung to "Take Me Out to the Ball Game")

Let's all go to the classroom,
It's time—just look at the clock.
First make a painting and wear a smock,
Then build a skyscraper block by block!
School is fun, the time goes so quickly,
The clock goes tick-tock, tick-tock.
And then soon it's time to go home—
Just look at the clock!

Plop and Flop!

(sung to "Old MacDonald Had a Farm")

We had some milk and spilled a drop.
It's time to get the mop!
Then all the pudding spilled on top.
It landed with a plop!

With a glop right here,
Get the mop right there!
Here a glop, there a plop,
Everywhere a glop plop,

Mop and sop up every drop,
Oops, I'm slipping—FLOP!

25 Fun Word Family Songs Sung to Favorite Tunes © 2013 by Pamela Chanko, Scholastic Teaching Resources

My Dog Spot

(sung to "Bingo")

I have a dog, his name is Spot,
And Spot has got a dot.
Spot has got a dot!
Spot has got a dot!
Spot has got a dot!
Yes, Spot has got a dot.

And Spot sleeps on my cot a lot,
He curls up in a knot.
Curls up in a knot!
Curls up in a knot!
Curls up in a knot!
Spot curls up in a knot.

My dog Spot does not get hot,
He loves to run and trot.
Loves to run and trot!
Loves to run and trot!
Loves to run and trot!
Spot loves to run and trot.

If You See a Little Duck

(sung to "London Bridge Is Falling Down")

If you see a little duck
And it's stuck
In the muck,
Pluck it up and hear it cluck.
Good luck, Duck!

Clean up all that messy muck,
Tuck that duck
In your truck.
Take it home and name it Chuck.
Good luck, Duck!

25 Fun Word Family Songs Sung to Favorite Tunes © 2013 by Pamela Chanko, Scholastic Teaching Resources

Bug in a Jug

(sung to "Mary Had a Little Lamb")

If you see a little bug
Looking snug
In a rug,
Shrug and give that bug a tug
And put it in a jug.

But next time that you use that jug,
Don't forget,
There's a bug!
Do not pour it in a mug
And do not take a glug!

Jump and Pump!

(sung to "If You're Happy and You Know It")

To keep your body healthy, give a jump!
To keep your body healthy, give a jump!
Don't sit there like a lump,
Don't let your shoulders slump.
To keep your body healthy, give a jump!

Now get your arms up high and give a pump!
Now get your arms up high and give a pump!
You don't want to be a grump,
Come on, get up and jump.
Now get your arms up high and give a pump!

Now stamp and tap your feet and hear them thump!
Now stamp and tap your feet and hear them thump!
Give your hips a little bump,
You won't turn into a grump—
You'll be healthy, and you'll want to give a jump!

25 Fun Word Family Songs Sung to Favorite Tunes © 2013 by Pamela Chanko, Scholastic Teaching Resources

What Was in the Trunk?

(sung to "Ten Little Indians")

Oh, the stuff in the trunk went clunk, plunk, clunk!
Oh, the stuff in the trunk went clunk, plunk, clunk!
Oh, the stuff in the trunk went clunk, plunk, clunk!
So much stuff in the trunk!

We opened the trunk—it stunk, stunk, stunk!
We opened the trunk—it stunk, stunk, stunk!
We opened the trunk—it stunk, stunk, stunk!
Oh, how that trunk stunk!

We cleaned out the junk, chunk by chunk!
We cleaned out the junk, chunk by chunk!
We cleaned out the junk, chunk by chunk!
We cleaned out that whole trunk!

Then out of the trunk something slunk!
Then out of the trunk something slunk!
Then out of the trunk something slunk!
Something slunk from the trunk!

And guess what it was? A little skunk!
That's what it was, a little skunk!
Yes, that's what it was, a little skunk!
That's what stunk in the trunk!

25 Fun Word Family Songs Sung to Favorite Tunes © 2013 by Pamela Chanko, Scholastic Teaching Resources

ack

back

"Jack's Snack"

black

Jack

"Jack's Snack"

pack

rack

"Jack's Snack"

sack

snack

"Jack's Snack"

25 Fun Word Family Songs Sung to Favorite Tunes © 2013 by Pamela Chanko, Scholastic Teaching Resources

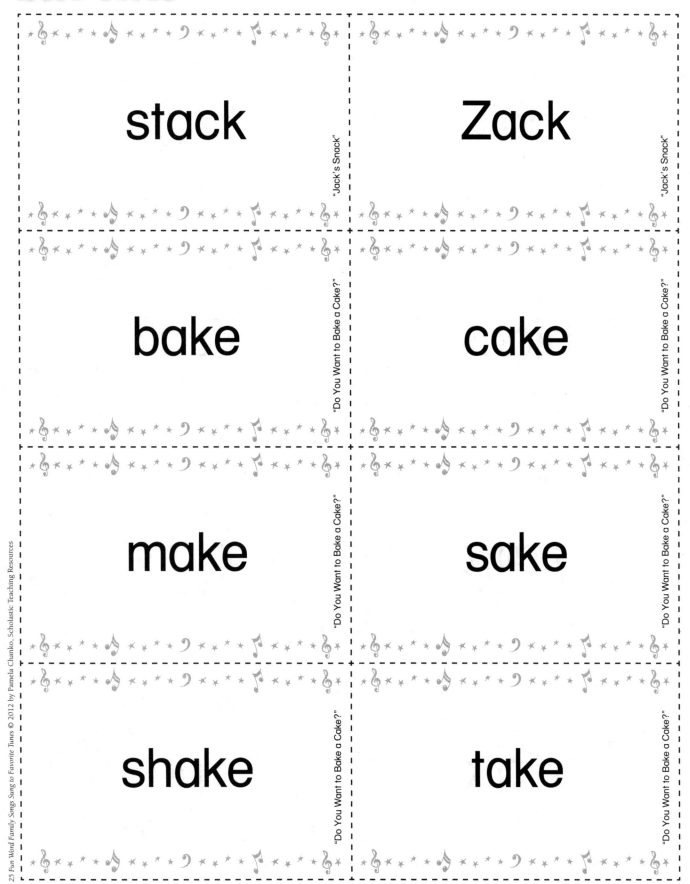

stack

Zack

"Jack's Snack"

bake

cake

"Do You Want to Bake a Cake?"

make

sake

"Do You Want to Bake a Cake?"

shake

take

"Do You Want to Bake a Cake?"

25 Fun Word Family Songs Sung to Favorite Tunes © 2012 by Pamela Chanko, Scholastic Teaching Resources

can

Dan

"Stan and Fran's Van"

fan

Fran

"Stan and Fran's Van"

man

pan

"Stan and Fran's Van"

plan

ran

"Stan and Fran's Van"

25 Fun Word Family Songs Sung to Favorite Tunes © 2013 by Pamela Chanko, Scholastic Teaching Resources

Word Cards

Stan

van

clap

flap

lap

nap

rap

slap

Word Cards

snap

"The Snap Tap, Clap Flap Rap"

tap

"Flash and Crash"

wrap

"The Snap-Tap, Clap-Flap Rap"

crash

"Flash and Crash"

dash

"Flash and Crash"

flash

"Flash and Crash"

thrash

"Flash and Crash"

splash

"Flash and Crash"

25 Fun Word Family Songs Sung to Favorite Tunes © 2013 by Pamela Chanko, Scholastic Teaching Resources

Word Cards

cat

chat

"Cat, Rat, Gnat!"

fat

flat

"Cat, Rat, Gnat!"

gnat

hat

"Cat, Rat, Gnat!"

pat

rat

"Cat, Rat, Gnat!"

25 Fun Word Family Songs Sung to Favorite Tunes © 2012 by Pamela Chanko, Scholastic Teaching Resources

sat

scat

"Cat, Rat, Gnat!"

"Cat, Rat, Gnat!"

slat

splat

"Cat, Rat, Gnat!"

"Cat, Rat, Gnat!"

that

ate

"Cat, Rat, Gnat!"

"Kate and Tate"

date

hate

"Kate and Tate"

"Kate and Tate"

25 Fun Word Family Songs Sung to Favorite Tunes © 2013 by Pamela Chanko, Scholastic Teaching Resources

Word Cards

gate

"Kate and Tate"

Kate

"Kate and Tate"

late

"Kate and Tate"

plate

"Kate and Tate"

rate

"Kate and Tate"

skate

"Kate and Tate"

state

"Kate and Tate"

Tate

"Kate and Tate"

day

gray

"A Day to Play"

play

ray

"A Day to Play"

say

spray

"A Day to Play"

stay

way

"A Day to Play"

25 Fun Word Family Songs Sung to Favorite Tunes © 2013 by Pamela Chanko, Scholastic Teaching Resources

Word Cards

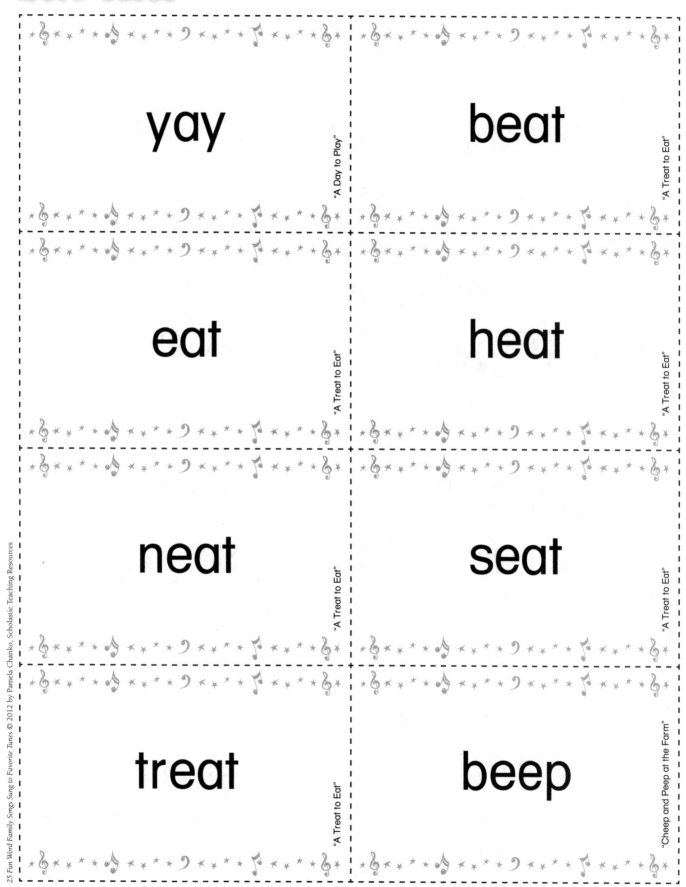

yay

"A Day to Play"

beat

"A Treat to Eat"

eat

"A Treat to Eat"

heat

"A Treat to Eat"

neat

"A Treat to Eat"

seat

"A Treat to Eat"

treat

"A Treat to Eat"

beep

"Cheep and Peep at the Farm"

cheep

creep

deep

keep

jeep

peep

sheep

sleep

25 Fun Word Family Songs Sung to Favorite Tunes © 2013 by Pamela Chanko, Scholastic Teaching Resources

Word Cards

steep

"Cheep and Peep at the Farm"

bell

"The Shop in the Dell"

dell

"The Shop in the Dell"

sell

"The Shop in the Dell"

shell

"The Shop in the Dell"

smell

"The Shop in the Dell"

swell

"The Shop in the Dell"

tell

"The Shop in the Dell"

25 Fun Word Family Songs Sung to Favorite Tunes © 2012 by Pamela Chanko, Scholastic Teaching Resources

well

"The Shop in the Dell"

yell

"The Shop in the Dell"

best

"The Best Nest"

chest

"The Best Nest"

nest

"The Best Nest"

pest

"The Best Nest"

rest

"The Best Nest"

test

"The Best Nest"

25 Fun Word Family Songs Sung to Favorite Tunes © 2013 by Pamela Chanko, Scholastic Teaching Resources

Word Cards

mice

"Three Nice Mice"

nice

"Three Nice Mice"

price

"Three Nice Mice"

rice

"Three Nice Mice"

slice

"Three Nice Mice"

spice

"Three Nice Mice"

twice

"Three Nice Mice"

glide

"Slide, Glide, and Ride!"

25 Fun Word Family Songs Sung to Favorite Tunes © 2012 by Pamela Chanko, Scholastic Teaching Resources

Word Cards

hide

ride

"Slide, Glide, and Ride!"

"Slide, Glide, and Ride!"

side

slide

"Slide, Glide, and Ride!"

"Slide, Glide, and Ride!"

wide

bright

"Slide, Glide, and Ride!"

"My Night-Light"

fright

light

"My Night-Light"

"My Night-Light"

25 Fun Word Family Songs Sung to Favorite Tunes © 2013 by Pamela Chanko, Scholastic Teaching Resources

night

"My Night-Light"

right

"My Night-Light"

sight

"My Night-Light"

tight

"My Night-Light"

bill

"Jill's Dollar Bill"

Bill

"Jill's Dollar Bill"

chill

"Jill's Dollar Bill"

fill

"Jill's Dollar Bill"

Word Cards

hill

Jill

"Jill's Dollar Bill"

"Jill's Dollar Bill"

still

thrill

"Jill's Dollar Bill"

"Jill's Dollar Bill"

Will

dine

"Jill's Dollar Bill"

"Will You Be a Friend of Mine?"

fine

line

"Will You Be a Friend of Mine?"

"Will You Be a Friend of Mine?"

25 Fun Word Family Songs Sung to Favorite Tunes © 2013 by Pamela Chanko, Scholastic Teaching Resources

mine	nine
"Will You Be a Friend of Mine?"	"Will You Be a Friend of Mine?"
pine	shine
"Will You Be a Friend of Mine?"	"Will You Be a Friend of Mine?"
cling	sing
"Sing of Spring!"	"Sing of Spring!"
spring	sting
"Sing of Spring!"	"Sing of Spring!"

25 Fun Word Family Songs Sung to Favorite Tunes © 2012 by Pamela Chanko, Scholastic Teaching Resources

string	**swing**
"Sing of Spring!"	*"Sing of Spring!"*
thing	**wing**
"Sing of Spring!"	*"Sing of Spring!"*
block	**clock**
"The School Clock"	*"The School Clock"*
smock	**tock**
"The School Clock"	*"The School Clock"*

25 Fun Word Family Songs Sung to Favorite Tunes © 2013 by Pamela Chanko, Scholastic Teaching Resources

drop

"Plop and Flop!"

flop

"Plop and Flop!"

glop

"Plop and Flop!"

mop

"Plop and Flop!"

plop

"Plop and Flop!"

sop

"Plop and Flop!"

top

"Plop and Flop!"

cot

"My Dog Spot"

dot

"Plop and Flop!"

got

"My Dog Spot"

hot

"My Dog Spot"

knot

"My Dog Spot"

lot

"My Dog Spot"

not

"My Dog Spot"

Spot

"My Dog Spot"

trot

"My Dog Spot"

25 Fun Word Family Songs Sung to Favorite Tunes © 2013 by Pamela Chanko, Scholastic Teaching Resources

Word Cards

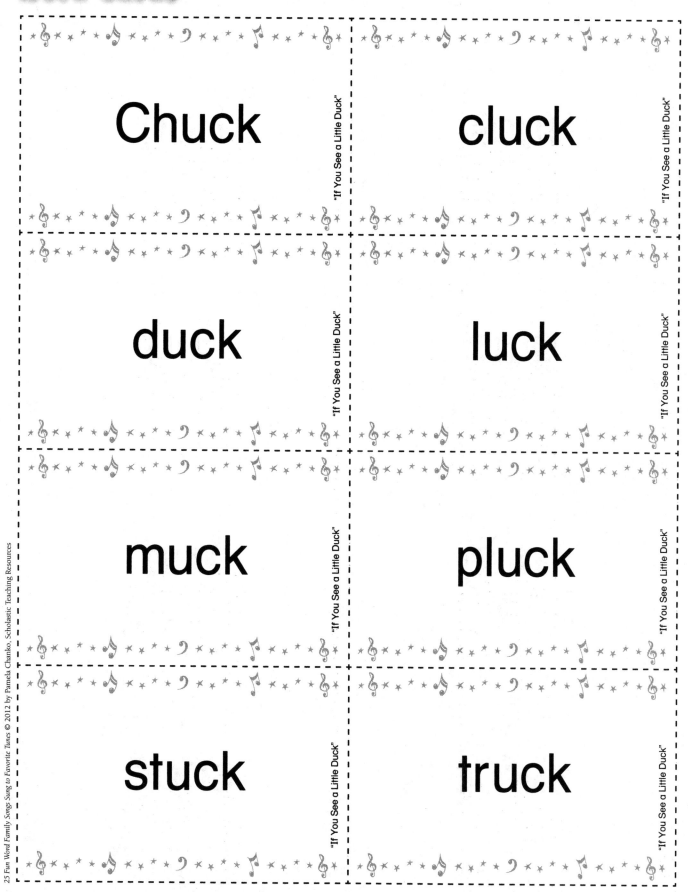

Chuck

"If You See a Little Duck"

cluck

"If You See a Little Duck"

duck

"If You See a Little Duck"

luck

"If You See a Little Duck"

muck

"If You See a Little Duck"

pluck

"If You See a Little Duck"

stuck

"If You See a Little Duck"

truck

"If You See a Little Duck"

tuck

bug

glug

jug

mug

rug

shrug

snug

Word Cards

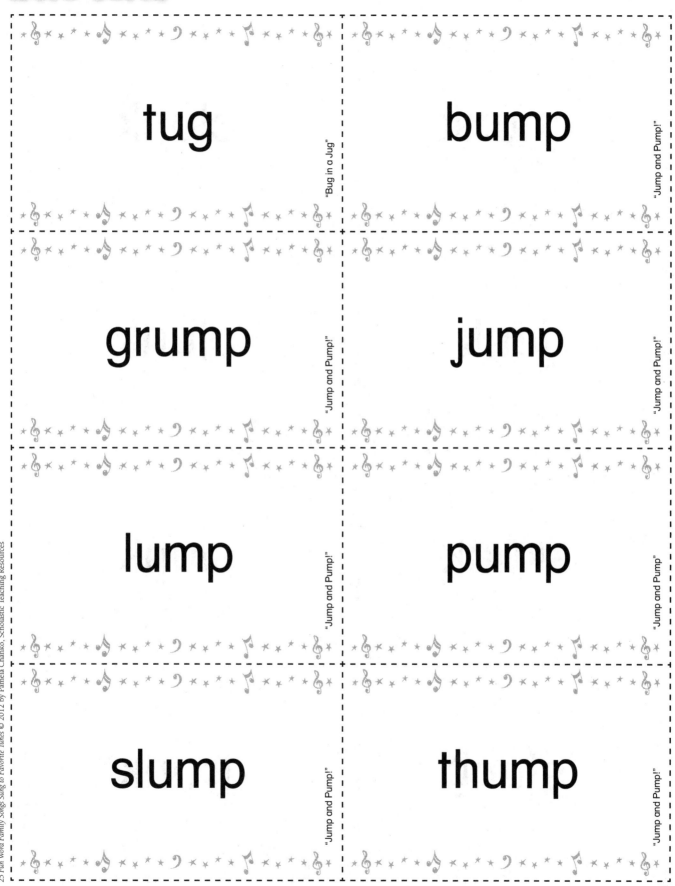

tug

"Bug in a Jug"

bump

"Jump and Pump!"

grump

"Jump and Pump!"

jump

"Jump and Pump!"

lump

"Jump and Pump!"

pump

"Jump and Pump!"

slump

"Jump and Pump!"

thump

"Jump and Pump!"

chunk

"What Was in the Trunk?"

clunk

"What Was in the Trunk?"

junk

"What Was in the Trunk?"

plunk

"What Was in the Trunk?"

skunk

"What Was in the Trunk?"

slunk

"What Was in the Trunk?"

stunk

"What Was in the Trunk?"

trunk

"What Was in the Trunk?"

25 Fun Word Family Songs Sung to Favorite Tunes © 2013 by Pamela Chanko, Scholastic Teaching Resources

Phonogram Cards

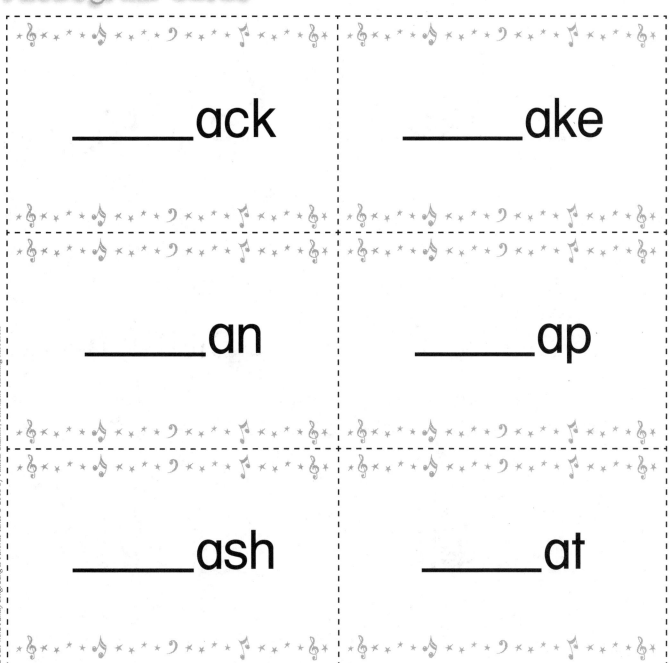

_____ack

_____ake

_____an

_____ap

_____ash

_____at

25 Fun Word Family Songs Sung to Favorite Tunes © 2013 by Pamela Chanko, Scholastic Teaching Resources

_____ate

_____ay

_____eat

_____eep

_____ell

_____est

25 Fun Word Family Songs Sung to Favorite Tunes © 2013 by Pamela Chanko, Scholastic Teaching Resources

Phonogram Cards

_____ice

_____ide

_____ight

_____ill

_____ine

_____ing

_____ock

_____op

_____ot

_____uck

_____ug

_____ump

_____unk

25 Fun Word Family Songs Sung to Favorite Tunes © 2013 by Pamela Chanko, Scholastic Teaching Resources

Word-Family Word Lists

-ack words	**-ap words**	**-ate words**	**-eep words**
clack	cap	crate	bleep
crack	chap	fate	seep
hack	gap	grate	sweep
knack	map	mate	weep
lack	sap	Nate	
Mack	scrap	slate	
quack	strap		**-ell words**
shack	trap		cell
slack	yap	**-ay words**	dwell
smack		bay	fell
tack		clay	jell
track	**-ash words**	fray	Nell
whack	bash	hay	spell
	brash	jay	
	cash	lay	
-ake words	clash	may	**-est words**
brake	gash	nay	crest
drake	hash	pay	jest
fake	lash	pray	lest
flake	mash	slay	quest
Jake	rash	stray	vest
lake	sash	sway	west
quake	slash	tray	wrest
rake	smash		zest
snake	stash		
stake	trash	**-eat words**	
wake		bleat	**-ice words**
		cheat	dice
	-at words	cleat	lice
-an words	bat	feat	splice
ban	brat	meat	thrice
bran	drat	peat	vice
clan	mat	pleat	
scan	spat	wheat	
span	vat		
tan			
than			

25 Fun Word Family Songs Sung to Favorite Tunes © 2013 by Pamela Chanko, Scholastic Teaching Resources

Word-Family Word Lists

-*ide* words	-*ine* words	-*op* words	-*ump* words
bride	shrine	bop	chump
chide	spine	chop	clump
pride	swine	cop	dump
snide	twine	crop	frump
stride	vine	pop	hump
tide	whine	prop	plump
	wine	shop	rump
		slop	stump
			trump

-*ight* words	-*ing* words
blight	bing
fight	bring
flight	ding
knight	fling
might	king
plight	ping
	ring

-*ot* words

blot	
clot	**-*unk* words**
jot	bunk
plot	drunk
pot	dunk
rot	flunk
shot	hunk
slot	shrunk
tot	spunk
	sunk

-*ill* words		
dill		
drill		
frill		
gill		
grill		
kill		
mill		
pill		
quill		
sill		
skill		
spill		
till		
trill		
twill		

-*ock* words	-*uck* words
crock	buck
dock	puck
flock	struck
frock	suck
hock	yuck
knock	
lock	
mock	**-*ug* words**
rock	chug
shock	drug
sock	dug
stock	hug
	lug
	plug
	pug
	slug
	smug
	thug

25 Fun Word Family Songs Sung to Favorite Tunes © 2013 by Pamela Chanko, Scholastic Teaching Resources